GUSTAV

MESSERSCHMITT 109 G (PART 1)

by Thomas H. Hitchcock

Recognizing the need to meet ever increasing altitude and speed demands, in 1940 the Messerschmitt company advanced plans for an improved Bf 109 to replace its Bf 109F. The new model was formulated around the DB 605 engine then being developed by Daimler-Benz. Within higher circles this new model was thought of as only a stopgap fighter awaiting introduction of more advanced models. However, as events soon proved, this "stopgap" development steadily became the standard fighter which outfitted more Luftwaffe squadrons than any other fighter type.

Before Gustav production could begin, deliveries of the DB 605 had to be guaranteed. During July 1940 a special Bf 109F airframe (W.Nr5604, VK +AB) was modified to incorporate short span wings and an early example of the DB 605. Although this development aircraft was allocated for comparison trials involving the Bf 109X, it served to evaluate the merits of the new Daimler-Benz engine.

Over the next fifteen months, development of the DB 605 lagged behind expectations. Therefore, flight-cleared DB 605 units were not forthcoming when an initial batch of twelve examples of the **Bf 109 G-0** were completed in October 1941. Pending availability of the DB 605, these airframes were mated initially with the older DB 601E as evaluation and test aircraft.

Bf 109 G-0 Aircraft:

W.Nr. 14 001 VJ +WA	W.Nr. 13 441 CC +ZP
W.Nr. 14 002 VJ +WB	W.Nr. 13 442 CC +ZQ
W.Nr. 14 003 VJ +WC	W.Nr. 13 448 BC +VK
W.Nr. 13 438 CC +ZM	W.Nr. 13 496 BC +VS
W.Nr. 13 439 CC +ZN	W.Nr. 13·500 BC +VW
W.Nr. 13 440 CC +ZO	W.Nr. 13 506 BJ +WC

The DB 605 incorporated a redesigned cylinder block to maximize the bore, repositioned spark plugs and modified main bearings. Daimler-Benz engineers were able to increase the permissible rpm while altering valve timing. This increased the intake phase and improved the scavenging giving greater volumetric efficiency. By May 1942 the first Gustav,

Resplendent after complete retoration, NASM Bf 109 G-6 is a supurb example of what is possible.

1

The First Gustav, W.Nr. 14 001, VJ +WA, was powered initially by the older DB 601E. This aircraft was retained by Messerschmitt as a test vehicle.

The third Gustav, W.Nr. 14 003, VJ +WC, fitted with a DB 605 A-1, W.Nr. 76 172, evaluated the unique butterfly tail assembly between March 2-18, 1943.

W.Nr. 14 001, had been re-engined with the DB 605 A-1, W.Nr. 76 233, to partipate in a multitude of engine and airframe tests during early summer 1942, and most objections were overcome.

Cabin pressurization also was developed for the Gustav although the majority were destined not to receive this equipment. Underwing wheel well covers were not fitted although the wells were suitably designed to accept a hinged door.

The decision to adopt the smoothly contoured spinner of the Me 210 in place of the originally proposed blunt tip model was reached when it was realized that the proposed MG FF cannon would not be adopted for engine installation.

Official aircraft handbooks routinely referred to the overall length of the Bf 109G as 8940 mm (29 ft-3 7/8 in) when, in fact, the true length of each was 9020 mm (29 ft-7 1/8 in). This inconsistency was the result of dimensions taken from drawings of aircraft with the proposed blunt spinner. In spite of delays the first production Gustav began leaving assembly lines during March 1942. The initial production model, **Bf 109 G-1,** was pressurized and powered by the DB 605 A-1, DB 605 B-1 or the DB 605 C-1 (each with a different gear ratio) driving a VDM 9-12087 3-bladed propellor.

Radio equipment was identical to that carried by the earlier Bf 109 F-4 and comprised an FuG 7a and FuG 25. Armament also was patterned after the Bf 109 F-4 consisting of an engine-mounted 20 mm MG 151/20 cannon (200 rounds) and two cowl-mounted 7.9 mm MG 17 machine guns (500 rpg). Late in May 1942 the first operational unit to receive the Gustav was 11./JG 2 "Richthofen," a special high altitude interceptor unit created from elements of 1./JG 2.

Bf 109 G-1, W.Nr. 14 250, CC +PU, being rolled out followed completion during the spring of 1943.

Bf 109 G-1, — — +UO, awaiting delivery to an operational unit in standard factory camouflage colors.

Bf 109 G-1/R6, — — +EL, operational in the East and displaying a coat of distemper white camouflage paint.

One of the first operational action reports is dated July 31, 1942. On this day 1./JG 2 became involved in combat with RAF Spitfires. During this battle the wingman of the Staffelkapitän, Oblt. Rudolf Pflanz, Feldwebel Grüber was forced to bail out. Pflanz, still under the impression that Grüber was guarding his tail, attacked and shot down a Spitfire to register his fifty-second victory. Seconds later he himself was shot down by another Spitfire, his aircraft catching fire and exploding at 15.05 hours south of Moncheau near

Abbeville, France. Oblt. Pflanz was flying a Bf 109 G-1, W. Nr. 10 318. On August 19, 1942, two additional Bf 109 G-1 models were lost to enemy action: the aircraft of Stabsfw. E. Kley, assigned to 1./JG 2, and that of Oblt. J. Schmidt, attached to 11./JG 26. Soon thereafter most Bf 109-equipped units began receiving the new Gustav, and by the end of 1942 it had all but replaced the Bf 109F as front-line equipment. The last reported loss of Bf 109 G-1 due to enemy action occurred near the end of the war on February 1,

1945, when W. Nr. 166 360, "Green 2" of 3./(Erg) JG 1 was shot down. This aircraft was attached to a semioperational training unit.

The Bf 109 G-1 was an excellent performer. Its introduction helped the Luftwaffe regain a measure of balance between itself and the potent Spitfire. Numerous tests were conducted in an effort to establish the potentialities and relative weaknesses of each fighter. On June 29, 1943, a

Newly completed Bf 109 G-1 models awaiting acceptance flights, present an impressive lineup. Note the subtle differences in markings.

Bf 109 G-2, BD +GC, shown here under test at Stendal.

Bf 109 G-2, BD +GP, one of a group of newly completed Gustavs.

standard Bf 109 G-1 was matched against a Focke-Wulf FW 190 A-5. The Gustav showed better climbing speed and time above critical altitude, but under critical altitude was inferior to the Focke-Wulf. Production of the **Bf 109 G-2** proceeded simultaneously with that of the Bf 109 G-1. Apart from the nonpressurized cabin, this model was identical to the G-1 series, but was produced in greater numbers. The service introduction of the Bf 109 G-2 extended through most Bf 109 units as rapidly as production would allow.

One of the earliest combat losses of the type occured on October 16, 1942, when Offz. H. Golinski of 3./JG 53 was lost while flying "Yellow 1," W. Nr. 10 582. A few days later on October 29, 1942, Hptm. W. D. Huy, posted to 7./JG 77, was reported lost while flying Bf 109 G-2, "White 1," W. Nr. 13 633. Lt. W. Crinius, of 3./JG 53, was shot down on January 13, 1943, while flying a Bf 109 G-2/R1 "chevron," W. Nr. 10 805.

The **Bf 109 Ga-1** and **Bf 109 Ga-2** variants were fitted with minor electrical changes

and intended for export. (a=ausland/ foreign). See p. 29. Soon after the service introduction of the Gustav, several squadrons began reporting mysterious fires shortly after takeoff, often resulting in loss

Fw. Helmut Maul posing with his mascot atop his Bf 109 G-2 while assigned to JG 1.

of the aircraft. On September 30, 1942, the famous "Star of Africa," Hptm. Hans Marseille, Staffelkapitan of 3./JG 27 experienced a mysterious engine fire over Egypt forcing him to bail out of his Bf 109 G-2/trop, W. Nr. 14 256. Although Marseille lost his life, others were able to para-

chute to safety. During prolonged ground running the DB 605 exhibited a tendency to overheat. This caused the horseshoe-shaped nose oil tank to seep oil over the hot engine, reaching a critical flash point shortly after takeoff. The remedy was to redesign the oil tank adding four small cooling airscoops to the forward cowling.

As production of the Gustav gained momentum, tests were conducted with unusual weapons systems. One example involved installation of two rearward firing MG 17s in a detachable container beneath the fuselage. Known as the Bf 109 G-2/WT 17 (Waffentropfen 17), it did not perform well and was not further developed. Two examples of a Bf 109 G-2 survive: one in England and another in Yugoslavia. The Yugoslavian example came from Bulgaria at the end of WW II and was flown briefly by the Yugoslavian Air Force as a trainer. The other machine, Bf 109 G-2/trop, W. Nr. 10 639, is currently at RAF Northolt awaiting restoration. Captured by British Forces in the Mediterranian area during late 1943, it arrived at RAF Collyweston on December 26 1943, for duties with No 1426 Flight.

It is believed that both photographs depict Bf 109 G-2/trop, W.Nr. 10639, now undergoing restoration in England. The photo to the left illustrates an unusual rear fuselage insignia of a black circle enclosing a white "X." This is believed to have been the unit marking of I./JG 77.

Brought down by ground fire, this Bf 109 G-2/trop was attached to 2./JG 27, one of the leading North African Luftwaffe fighter units. A British soldier is examining the cowl machine **gun electrical** components.

On **Februa**ry 8, 1944, it was ground-run **after** reassembly, and eleven days later it was flown again, still in original German markings. However, by February 25, 1944, it had been repainted and flown in RAF markings carrying the Air Ministry code RN 228. Although conclusive evidence is lacking, it is believed that this aircraft was originally "Yellow 6" flown by I./JG 77 and is illustrated by the photograph at the bottom of page 4. Limited production of the **Bf 109 G-3** was initiated during August 1943 following service introduction of the Bf 109 G-4. Although few G-3 models were completed, 11./JG 26 did receive examples during this period. Ofw. H. Hoffman flew "Red 7," W. Nr. 20 225 operationally with that unit during August. The Bf 109 G-3 was pressurized and fitted with similar armament as the Bf 109 G-1. Radio equipment was altered to include the FuG 16Z and FuG 25, while the specific engine was the DB 605A-1. In order respects it was nearly identical to the similarly pressurized Bf 109 G-1.

As loaded weight had increased, it was found that the tires were becoming insufficient to accommodate demands. Resultingly, during August 1942 the Continental, Metzeler and Dunlop tire manufacturers, recommended that the Gustav be fitted with the 660 × 160 mainwheels (replacing 650 × 150) and the 350 × 135 (replacing 290 × 110) tailwheel. In accordance

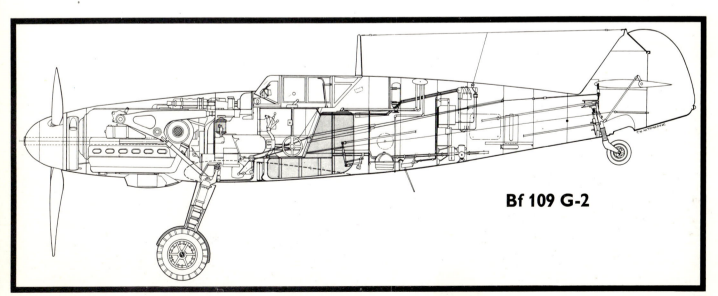

Bf 109 G-2

Bf 109 G-3, "Black 3," — — +YS, was one of the relatively few aircraft of this type completed.

Hptm. Johannes Steinhoff, Kommandeur of 11./JG 52 prepares for another sortie in his Bf 109 G-3.

with these recommendations, all models of the Bf 109 G-3, most Bf 109 G-4 models and a few Bf 109 G-2 models received the larger tires. The slightly larger main-wheel resulted in the previously smooth upper wing surface being interrupted by a bulged fairing to enclose the otherwise protruding tire. Although the tailwheel of the Gustav was intended to be retractable, with the enlarged tire it usually was made nonretractable.

Preceeding the Bf 109 G-3 on the production line, the nonpressurized **Bf 109 G-4** entered production during April 1943.

Apart from the lack of pressurization equipment it was similar to the G-3 series. The Bf 109 G-4 series received the DB 605 A-1 power-plant as standard, with armament identical to previous models. The **Bf 109 G-4/U1** was equipped with the Me P 6 reversible-pitch prop. **Bf 109 Ga-4** was the export designation.

The first unit to take delivery of the Bf 109 G-4 was 1./JG 27 on January 26, 1943, at Evreux, France. By February 20, 1943, 1./JG 27 was fully operational with G-4s commanded by Hauptmann Heinrich Setz. On March 13, 1943, after downing three

Spitfires in rapid order, Gruppen, Kommanduer Setz piloting a Bf 109 G-4, W.Nr. 14 862, was shot down by another Spitfire. By this time most other frontline Bf 109 units were outfitted with the Bf 109 G-4 including reconnaissance units such as 2.(F)/123. Oblt R. Rapp of 2.(F)/123 was reported lost while flying a Bf 109 G-4, 4U +KW on April 29, 1943. Early in July 1943 at the time of "Operation Citadel," III./JG 52 was equipped with the Bf 109 G-4. At the same time III./JG 3 was flying examples of the Bf 109 G-6. On July 5, 1943, Fw. W. Hauswirth of 8./JG 52 was

Bf 109 G-4/trop "Black 13" of 1./JG 27 being given the red, white, and blue of the new owners. Although operational in North Africa, this example clearly retains its European camouflage coloring.

Taken somewhere in Italy, this Bf 109 G-4/R6, VG +——, is receiving an electrical boost prior to takeoff.

lost flying a Bf 109 G-4, "Black 8," W.Nr. 19 754, while participating in "Operation Citadel." One of the last recorded Bf 109 G-4s lost during the war was "Yellow 2," W.Nr. 16 291, of 11./JG 26 on February 24, 1944.

In January 1944 the pressurized **Bf 109 G-5** began to enter service powered by the DB 605 A-1. The distinguishing features, twin "Beule" bulges on the cowl, were made necessary by the larger 13 mm MG 131 machine gun feed chutes. This Rheinmetall-Borsig weapon weighed 40 lb (18 kg) having a rate of fire of 960 rpm compared with the 28 lb (12.6 kg) MG 17 which offered a 1000 rpm. Total ammunition

carried by the Bf 109 G-5 consisted of 300 rpg for each MG 131 plus 200 rounds for the Mauser-designed MG 151/20 cannon. The latter weapon weighed 93.5 lb (42 kg) and had a capability of 780 rpm. Radio equipment consisted of a FuG 16Z and the newer FuG 25a. The tall radio mast was fitted to early production G-5s but with the "R7" kit, the short mast and direction-finding loop were standard. Pilot protection was increased by addition of the Gallandpanzer (bullet-resistant glass mated to thicker armor plating for the canopy hood). Additionally, a new one-piece clear canopy, the Erla Haube, was available on some G-5s. This one-piece canopy was mated with "Gallandpanzer"

offering greater visibility and pilot protection. Production G-5s and G-6s were eligible to receive the newly introduced wooden tailplane. This modification bearing no special designation, was evaluated during January 1943 by the Fokker concern at Antwerp.

During April and May 1942 tests were initiated to improve the flying qualities of the Gustav. Two aircraft were selected as test vehicles: Bf 109F, W.Nr. 5716 and Bf 109 G-0, W.Nr. 14 001. Both were fitted with wing ailerons containing an inset fixed Flettner trim tab and a re-designed rudder reducing the mass balance horn to a minimum.

Bf 109 G-5/U2/R6, "Yellow 5" With Unteroffizier Hans Seyringer. Soon after this photograph was taken early in February 1944, Uffz. Seyringer was shot down by a P-51.

Hauptmann Gerhard Barkhorn's Bf 109 G-5/U2. Barkhorn, Gruppen Kommandeur of 11./JG 52 was Germany's second scoring ace with 301 confirmed victories.

The three photographs above graphically depict the cowl bulges necessitated by the larger MG 131 machine gun ammunition feed chutes. Note the asymetrical cowl hand grips on the Finnish Bf 109 G-6 (MT-509) to the left. Center photo depicts a standard Bf 109 G-6/R3 with the Erla Haube, while the photo to the right is of the NASM'S Bf 109 G-6.

RÜSTSÄTZE

Five Rüstsätze subtypes of the Bf 109 G-5 were authorized, although it is unlikely that all were completed. Other modifications to the Bf 109 G-5 included operational use of underwing air-to-air rockets. Although no "R" was designated, this version usually was listed as **Bf 109 G-5/BR 21** denoting the 21 cm Bord Rakete 21, "Dödel." It fired a projectile known as Wgr. 42, or on occasion, the 21 cm Nebelwerfer 42. Operations with this weapon system initially were carried out with the Bf 109 G-6 in autumn 1943. Elements of JG 1, JG 3, JG 26, and JG 27 operating against U.S.A.A.F. bombers achieved moderate success. The large

"Ofenrohr" tubes represented a significant drag factor and the system was not universally liked by pilots. Nevertheless, III./JG 3 based at Bad Wörshofen continued operations with the Bf 109 G-5/BR 21 during April 1944, again with limited success.

Although no examples of the Bf 109 G-5 are knwon to exist today, one example was captured and brought to Wright Field on January 20, 1945, bearing U.S. Army Air Corps Evaluation Branch code EB 109. On March 3 it was still created with 0 hours. Project engineer Brown and Crew Chief Terry were assigned to perform

assembly and a 50 hour inspection in Hanger 3 which was reserved for special equipment. By May 12 it was slated for storage, but by October 1, 1945, it was shipped to Freeman Field, Indiana. Presumably this plane was rendered surplus and assigned for salvage.

As recounted on page 20, the **Bf 109 G-5/AS** employed the DB 605 AS driving a metal VDM 9-12159A prop. The **Bf 109 G-5/U2/AS** received GM 1 powerboost in unison with the DB 605 ASC (C=C3 fuel) while the **Bf 109 G-5/R2/AS** was a photo-reconnaissance model powered by the DB 605 ASB (B=B4 fuel) without GM1.

AIRCRAFT	RÜSTSÄTZ	LOCATION	REMARKS
109 G-0/R3	1 × 300 Ltr aux fuel tank	underfuselage	Armor and armament not fitted to Bf 109 G-0 aircraft. Evaluation aircraft only.
109 G-1/R1	1 × ETC 500/IXb bomb rack	underfuselage	Service debut delayed of this fighter-bomber with few being completed.
109 G-1/R2	GM 1 powerboost	left wing	Lightweight fighter without armor and underwing cannon. 1 × 300 Ltr aux fuel tank.
109 G-1/R3	1 × 300 Ltr aux fuel tank	underfuselage	Fighter with extended range.
109 G-1/R6	2 × MG 151/20 cannon	underwing	Heavy fighter.
109 G-2/R1	1 × ETC 500/IXb bomb rack	underfuselage	Fighter-bomber with extended range. 2 × 300 aux fuel tanks, No MG 17, Production by Fieseler, Kassel.
109 G-2/R2	Rb 50/30 camera	fuselage	Reconnaissance-fighter with 1 × 300 aux fuel tank and no MG 151/20. Production by Erla, Leipzig.
109 G-2/R3	Rb 75/30 camera	fuselage	Reconnaissance-fighter with 2 × 300 aux fuel tanks and no MG 17 or underwing cannon.
109 G-2/R3	1 × 300 Ltr aux fuel tank	underfuselage	Fighter with extended range.
109 G-2/R4	Rb 50/30 camera	fuselage	Reconnaissance-fighter with 2 × 300 aux fuel tanks and no MG 17 or underwing cannon.
109 G-2/R6	2 × MG 151/20 cannon	underwing	Heavy fighter.
109 G-3/R1	1 × ETC 500/IXb bomb rack	underfuselage	Fighter-bomber. Service debut delayed, few completed as production not authorized.
109 G-3/R2	GM 1 powerboost	left wing	Lightweight fighter without armor, underwing cannon or bombs. 1 × 300 aux fuel tank (Bf 109 G-3/U2 was development).
109 G-3/R2	4 × ETC 50/VIIId bomb rack	underfuselage	Fighter-bomber. Production not initiated.
109 G-3/R3	1 × 300 Ltr aux fuel tank	underfuselage	Fighter with extended range. Extensive usage.
109 G-3/R6	2 × MG 151/20 cannon	underwing	Heavy fighter.
109 G-4/R1	1 × ETC 500/IXb bomb rack	underfuselage	Fighter-bomber. Limited service model.
109 G-4/R2	Rb 50/30 camera	fuselage	Reconnaissance-fighter with 1 × 300 aux fuel tank. No MG 151/20 cannon. Std reconn. model.
109 G-4/R2	4 × ETC 50/VIIId bomb rack	underfuselage	Fighter-bomber. Production not initiated.
109 G-4/R3	Rb 75/30 camera	fuselage	Reconnaissance-fighter with 2 × 300 aux fuel tanks. No MG 17 or bombs. Production not initiated.
109 G-4/R3	1 × 300 Ltr aux fuel tank	underfuselage	Fighter with extended range. Extensive usage.
109 G-4/R4	Rb 50/30 camera	fuselage	Reconnaissance-fighter with 2 × 300 aux fuel tanks and no MG 17 or underwing cannon. Production not initiated.
109 G-4/R6	2 × MG 151/20 cannon	underwing	Heavy fighter. Large scale service model.
109 G-4/R7	Peilrufanlage	fuselage	Direction-finding equipment installation. Fitted to some models.
109 G-5/R1	1 × ETC 500/IXb bomb rack	underfuselage	Fighter-bomber. Production not undertaken.
109 G-5/R2	GM 1 powerboost	left wing	Lightweight fighter without armor, underwing cannon, bombs or aux fuel tank. Developed into Bf 109 G-5/U2.
109 G-5/R2	4 × ETC 50/VIIId bomb rack	underfuselage	Fighter-bomber. Production not initiated.
109 G-5/R3	1 × 300 Ltr aux fuel tank	underfuselage	Fighter with extended range. Extensive usage.
109 G-5/R6	2 × MG 151/20 cannon	underwing	Heavy fighter. Extensive usage.
109 G-5/R7	Peilrufanlage	fuselage	Direction-finding equipment fitted to most models.
109 G-5/R1/AS	1 × ETC 500 XIb bomb rack	underfuselage	Fighter-bomber. Not applicable for G-5/U2 or G-5/R2. Production very limited.
109 G-5/R2/AS	Rb 50/30 camera	fuselage	Reconnaissance-fighter without engine cannon.
109 G-5/R3/AS	1 × 300 Ltr aux fuel tank	underfuselage	Fighter with extended range. Extensive usage.
109 G-5/R6/AS	2 × MG 151/20 cannon	underwing	Heavy fighter. Moderate usage.
109 G-5/R7/AS	Peilrufanlage	fuselage	Direction-finding equipment standard on most examples.
109 G-6/R1	1 × ETC 500/IXb bomb rack	underfuselage	Fighter-bomber. Production limited.
109 G-6/R2	4 × ETC 50/VIIId bomb rack	underfuselage	Fighter-bomber. Production not initiated.
109 G-6/R2	Rb 50/30 camera	fuselage	Reconnaissance-fighter with MW 50, 1 × 300 Ltr aux fuel tank. Extensive usage.
109 G-6/R3	Rb 75/30 camera	fuselage	Reconnaissance-fighter with 2 × 300 aux fuel tanks. No armor, MG 131, R6 or bombs. Production canceled.
109 G-6/R3	1 × 300 Ltr aux fuel tank	underfuselage	Fighter with extended range. Extensive usage.
109 G-6/R4	Rb 50/30 camera	fuselage	Reconnaissance-fighter with 2 × 300 aux fuel tanks. No armor, MG 131, R6 or bombs. Production canceled.
109 G-6/R6	2 × MK 108 cannon	underwing	Zerstörer-fighter with 2 30 mm underwing cannon. Few completed.
109 G-6/R6	2 × MG 151/20 cannon	underwing	Heavy fighter. Extensive usage.
109 G-6/R7	Peilrufanlage	fuselage	Direction-finding equipment fitted to most examples.
109 G-6/R1/AS	1 × ETC 500/XIb bomb rack	underfuselage	Fighter-bomber. Very limited production.
109 G-6/R3/AS	1 × 300 Ltr aux fuel tank	underfuselage	Fighter with extended range. Extensive usage.
109 G-6/R4/AS	2 × MK 108 cannon	underwing	Zerstörer-fighter with 2 30 mm underwing cannon. Few completed.
109 G-6/R6/AS	2 × MG 151/20 cannon	underwing	Heavy fighter. Limited usage.
109 G-6/R7/AS	Peilrufanlage	fuselage	Direction-finding equipment fitted to most examples.

ETC = Elektrische Trägervorrichtung für Cylinder bomben (Electrically operated carriers for cylinderical bombs.)
GM = Nitrous Oxide powerboost (See p.10.)
MG = Maschinengewehr (Machine gun)

MK = Maschinenkanone (Machine cannon)
MW = Methanol water powerboost (See p.10.)
Rb = Reihenbildkamera (Automatic photoreconnaissance camera)

Bf 109 G-2/R1, BD +GC

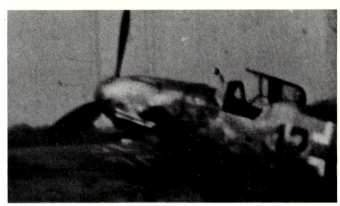

Bf 109 G-5/R2/AS, 12 +5F

Bf 109 G-6/U2/R3, W.Nr. 412 951, "White 16."

Bf 109 G-6/U2/R3, W.Nr. 412 951, "TP 814."

Bf 109 G-6/R4

Bf 109 G-6/R6

Bf 109 G-6/R6 of Stab/JG 27 also fitted with Rüstsätz R3 and R7. Note green tail bond.

9

UMRÜST-BAUSÄTZE

Umrüst-Bausätze		G-0	G-1	G-2	G-3	G-4	G-5	G-5/AS	G-6	G-6/AS
U1	Me P 6 prop		●	●		●			●	
U2	GM 1		●		●	●	●	●	●	●
U3	MW								●	
U4	MK 108								●	●
U5	3 × MK 108								●	
U6	MK 103 (provisional)									●

Under the term Umrüst-Bausätze a number of factory modifications carried out became standard equipment, giving more altitude or increasing the chances for inexperienced pilots to bring down Allied aircraft.

U1 In 1942 Messerschmitt evaluated the Me P 6 reversible-pitch prop on various examples of the Bf 109 G-1, G-2, G-4, and G-6. One Bf 109 G-2/U1 was known to have been employed operationally in 1943 by Jasta

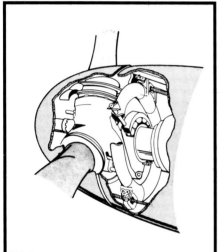

The Messerschmitt P6 prop was intended for both the DB 601 and the DB 605 engines.

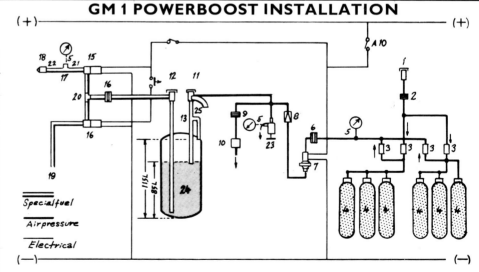

Bf 109 G-6/U2/U4 "Blue 29" of the 2nd Gruppe of an unknown training unit. Photographed in Germany in 1945, an American soldier is seen in the cockpit. Besides the unusual comouflage scheme, this aircraft is fitted with both GM 1 and the engine-mounted MK 108.

Helgoland. Formed on April 10, 1943, to counter growing U.S.A.A.F. attacks on Bremen, Kiel, and Emden, this unit took its name from the North Sea Island off the German coast. The principal advantage of the reversible-pitch prop is that it greatly reduces the landing roll when used in unison with wheel braking.

U2 This designation referred solely to addition of a powerboosting system known as GM1. Codenamed "haha" or "laughing gas" (colloquially: Göring Mischung Göring's Mixture), it was nitrous-oxide (N_2O) contained under pressure in liquid form and injected directly into the supercharger intake. This boosting system allowed the pilot to fly above the rated altitude for the DB 605. Nitrous-oxide provided the engine with additional oxygen for approximately 45 to 50 minutes at emergency boost pressure. It also acted as an antidetonant and served to increase power by a charge cooling effect. The fluid was contained in a 115 L (28 gal) cylindrical insulated tank immediately behind the pilot.

GM 1 POWERBOOST INSTALLATION

Special fuel
Air pressure
Electrical

1 Pressurized air filler	10 Safety valve	18 Nozzle
2 Pressurized air filter	11 Tank air valve	19 High speed blowoff line
3 Nonreturn valve	12 Tank filler	20 T-fitting
4 Pressurized air tanks	13 T-fitting +washer	21 Armored tube
5 Stop for pressure flow	14 GM 1 filter	22 Armored tube
6 Filter	15 Rate valve	23 Hand operated valve
7 Electrical high pressure valve	16 High speed blowoff valve	24 GM 1 container
8 Pressure reducer	17 T-fitting pressure	25 Flush washer
9 Filter	measurement	

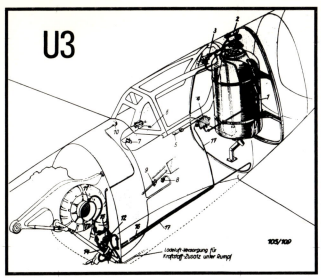

U3 The MW drawing shown left refers to the Bf 109 K-4, but is typical for MW installations utilized by the Bf 109 G-6, G-8, G-10 and G-14 series.

U4 Right: this drawing of the short barrel engine-mounted MK 108 refers to the Bf 109 G-6/U4 but is also typical for the G-10/U4 and G-14/U4.

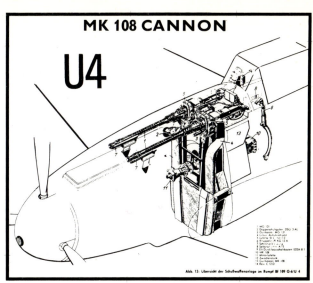

MK 108 CANNON

However, in the proposed Bf 109 G-3/R2 and G-5/R2, the GM 1 was to be contained in the port wing as it was in the Bf 109 F-4/Z. Six compressed air cylinders providing the necessary propellant pressure were contained within the right wing. The complete system weighed approximately 134 lb (60 kg) dry and 434 lb (195 kg) filled. In all models except the Bf 109 G-1, the filler cap for GM 1 was located on the upper right side of the fuselage opposite the main fuel filler hatch. With the Bf 109 G-5 and G-6 series an enlarged oil pump was fitted to the engine requiring the addition of a teardrop shaped bulge to the lower right cowl. Frequently the

by a yellow and white fuel triangle immediately below the filler hatch preventing possible confusion with the GM 1 while the underwing compressed air filler hatch was indicated by a blue marker.

U3 This designates a power-boost system known as MW (Methanol-Wasser) injection, more commonly MW 50. This referred to 50% Methanol (CH_3OH) and 49.5% tap water (H_2O) plus 0.5% Schutzöl 39 (anticorrosion fluid). A variant of this ratio was MW 30, which was 30% Methanol and 69.5% tap water plus 0.5% Schutzöl. The system was used to obtain extra power below the rated altitude of the supercharger and acted as an antidetonant, providing charge cooling and greater boost pressure. A 4% power increase could be obtained for a maximum of 10 continuous minutes, with 5 minutes lapse time between use periods. Spark plug life was cut to 15-30 hours while fuel consumption rose by 40% during takeoff.

The MW was contained within a 29 gal (118 L) cylindrical tank immediately behind the pilot. Boost pressure from the supercharger was used to apply the necessary propellant pressure which brought the solution to the supercharger intake where it was injected directly. The MW was controlled by a solenoid valve, actuated by an automatic throttle and a master switch in the cockpit. A pressure gauge also was fitted and the mixture was injected automatically when the throttle was fully open unless the master switch was turned off. Within this installation another power-boosting mixture known as EW 50 (Ethanol-Water) could have been carried. This mixture consisted of 50% ethyl alcohol and 49.5% tap water plus 0.5% Schutzöl 39. As in the case of the GM 1 powerboost, MW (or EW) powerboost was denoted by the filler hatch on the right side of the fuselage opposite the main fuel-filler point and by an enlarged oil pump enclosed by a teardrop fairing. Unlike GM 1, a vertically divided blue-white-blue triangle often was applied beneath the MW filler hatch preventing inadvertent confusion with the aft engine primer tank.

U4 This modification was restricted to the MK 108 engine-mounted 30 mm cannon. Mounted in place of the usual 20 mm MG 151/20 cannon, this weapon was introduced as the U4 modification toward late 1943. It was fitted to a substantial number of Bf 109 G-6 models. The MK 108, manufactured by Rheinmetall-Borsig, was a powerful weapon characterized by a steady slow rate of fire (Max. 450 rpm) and its simple construction (80% stamp-

ings). It was fired by electric ignition and was charged and triggered by compressed air. Two tanks containing the compressed air were located in the aft section of the fuselage and connected to the weapon by tubing. These compressed air tanks were filled at a small circular hatch located midway along the lower rear portion of the right fuselage. This filler hatch was identical to those found on early production Gustavs which were fitted with the cowl MG 17 weapons (G-1 through G-4), and which were similarly charged by compressed air. Only 65 rounds were carried for the MK 108 while the cowl MG 131 guns received 300 rounds. The MK 108 was loaded from inside the cockpit by means of a disintegrating belt from an ammunition can mounted above the weapon.

U5 This designator refered to the installation of three MK 108 cannons into one weapons system. During October 1943, a Bf 109 G-6, W.Nr. 440 005, was evaluated with both the R4 and U4 kits in combination. For various reasons this potent armament was not sanctioned for adoption.

U6 It is believed that this modification was associated with the 30 mm MK 103 engine-mounted cannon. Although research has failed to confirm this belief, circumstantial evidence supports its use under this designation. The MK 103, manufactured by Rheinmetall-Borsig, was another powerful weapon with a relatively slow rate of fire (Max. 420 rpm) incorporating a number of stampings. The Bf 109 G-14 (see CU 7) was eligible for the "U6" modification and it is possible that this item was evaluated previously by a Bf 109 G-6.

Bf 109 G-6/trop, KT +WE, found at Catania, Italy, August 6, 1943.

TROPICAL MODIFICATIONS

Although all of the Gustavs discussed within this title were eligible to receive "trop" equipment for service in North Africa or other sandy areas, in fact the pressurized Bf 109 G-1, G-3, G-5, and the AS-powered models did not receive this equipment on an operational basis.

Externally only three amendments were discernible: (1) a sand shield and cylindrical dust filter added to the supercharger air scoop, (2) two small brackets on the port side of the fuselage, and (3) whitewall tires. The clamshell sand-shield was opened after takeoff and closed prior to landing by means of a cable extending to a hand grip located on the lower left corner of the instrument panel. While on the

ground, air was drawn in through the fine wire mesh cylindrical dust filter attached to the lip of the supercharger air scoop

and supported by two braces attached to the port cowl. The two small brackets fastened directly to the fuselage port side

beneath the canopy and were intended to support hangers for a large sun parasol. Additionally, the main wheels were to be painted with a special white paint to reflect direct sunlight but this requirement appears to have been ignored by the majority.

Internal additions included special covers for the thermostats attached to the nose oil tank and radiator coolant tank as well as for the cylinders operating the underwing and nose radiator flaps. Emergency survival equipment was located within the space beneath and aft of the radio mast while a carbine and bracket were contained in the aft fuselage. Many of the Gustavs imported by Finland between 1943 and 1944 were fitted not only with the sand and dust filter, but many carried skis in the place of the carbine.

Bf 109 G-6, W.Nr. 165 450, MT-469, fitted with the "trop" sand filter in Finland.

Bf 109 G-6/trop of JG 53 fitted with the R6 kit.

Bf 109 G-6 belonging to the National Air and Space Museum.

Combat operations with the Bf 109 G-5 began six months after the service debut of the G-6 series. Most examples were fitted with GM 1 powerboost during manufacture, allowing a service ceiling advantage over the nonpressurized Bf 109 G-6. Lt. Wolfgang Gberfeld of 4./JG 11, flying a Bf 109 G-5/U2, "White 9," W.Nr. 110 027, was shot down on January 11, 1944. This was one of the first losses recorded for the Bf 109 G-5, followed on the same day by the loss of Gefr. H. Weitzel also of 4./JG 11, while flying his Bf 109 G-5/U2, "White 13," W.Nr. 110 004. Eighteen days later Bf 109 G-5/U2 "Yellow 10," W.Nr. 15 942 was shot down while being flown by Uffz. H. Schumann of 6./JG 11. The Bf 109 G-5 also participated in development programs for the Bf 109H and Me 209H.

From June 1943 to mid-1944 the **Bf 109 G-6** was produced in large numbers. Its appearance actually preeceded the G-5 models. Apart from the lack of cabin pressurization the G-6 series was identical to the G-5 series. A wide range of modification kits were available to equip the G-6 to perform specific roles. See p. 8. **Bf 109 G-6/U1** was a special fighter equipped with the Me P 6 reversible-pitch prop assembly. The **Bf 109 G-6/U2 and U3** were

aircraft equipped respectively with GM 1 and MW powerboosting systems. The **Bf 109 G-6/U4** was a Zerstörer fighter mounting a single 30 mm MK 108 cannon firing through the propellor spinner. Examples destined for export to Germany's allies were identified as the **Bf 109 Ga-6.**

By the end of 1943 operational use of the Bf 109 G-6 had extended through most of the Luftwaffe's day fighter forces. Clearly it was the workhorse of the fighters. Many aces preferred this model rather than other fighter types such as the Focke-Wulf FW 190. There can be no doubt that the G-6 was a supurb warplane; however, by 1944 it had been eclipsed by higher performing Allied types. It is recognized though, that the Bf 109 G-6 was responsible for more Allied aircraft losses than any

Close-up of the "Erla Haube."

other type. Varying operational needs caused the G-6 to be subjected to continual development studies. At various times it was tied to the Bf 109H program, the Bf 109 ST project and to the Bf 109Z twin, to name a few. The Erla-designed clearvision canopy was mounted on a substantial number during 1944, while the tall tailplane also often was incorporated as supplies permitted.

The Bf 109 G-6 also tested other modifications during 1943-1944, such as the 21 cm air-to-air rocket system. Known as the **Bf 109 G-6/BR 21**, several examples were fitted with the "Dödel" but operational use revealed unacceptable limitations.

As recounted on p.20, the G-6 was recipient of the improved DB 605 AS engine, receiving the designation **Bf 109 G-6/AS**. This special engine enabled the Gustav to reach an even higher altitude. The Bf 109 G-6/AS and the **Bf 109 G-6/U4/AS** received the DB 605 ASB engine (using B4/87 octane fuel) without powerboost while the **Bf 109 G-6/U2/AS** and **Bf 109 G-6/R4/AS** received the DB 605 ASC (using C3/96 octane fuel) with GM 1 powerboost. Three units employed the Bf 109 G-6/AS in Defense of the Reich during 1944, these being: III./JG 1, I./JG 5, and II./JG 11.

13

Bf 109 G-6/U2, W.Nr. 165 227, MT-452, now on permanent exhibit at Utti Air Force Base, Finland. Authentically restored in its wartime color scheme, Captain Hannu Valtonen was responsible for much painstaking work in this magnificent restoration.

Bf 109 G-6/U2, W.Nr. 163 824, was the personal property of the late Sidney Marshall who stored this Gustav at Bankstown, Australia. Most of the cockpit instruments of this particular example have, unfortunately, disappeared over the years.

Bf 109 G-6/Y, W.Nr. 167 271, MT-507, now on public display at Rissala Air Force Base, Finland. Like its sister aircraft, MT-452, it has been faithfully restored in its wartime camouflage and marking scheme. Note that the lengthened tail wheel leg appears on this Gustav. A number of Bf 109 G-6 models were fitted with this modification which was designed to improve ground handling.

Bf 109 G-6, W.Nr. 165 545, standing derelict amongst partially completed
Me 410 fuselages at Messerschmitt's Augsburg plant during May 1945.

During mid-1943 the Luftwaffe installed a network of ground control stations throughout Germany and the Low-Countries to coordinate fighter defenses. Known as the "Y system," it enabled ground control to bring fighters on an intercept course with a bomber force. The intercepting fighters would have one aircraft fitted with the "Y system," with others in reserve. Identified as a **Bf 109 G-6/Y**, this aircraft would receive continuous transmissions from a ground station informing the pilot of the position, course, and altitude of the bomber formation in addition to other factors such as enemy fighters, weather changes, etc. The "Y" aircraft pilot would then transmit this information on a different frequency to others within the flight, thus enabling ground control to place its fighters accurately on an intercept course. Immediately upon visual contact, control of the fighters was passed to the Geschwader

Kommodore (Group Commander) for the actual engagement. Aircraft fitted with the "Y system" received the FuG 16ZY radio coupled with the "Peilrufanlage" (R7 kit). Under the port wing a whip antenna, known as the Morane mast, was fitted which tied in directly to the FuG 16ZY. Within the cockpit there was a four-way setting on the radio:

Position I
 Y Führungsfrequenz or communications only for the Staffelführer with the Jagdführer.

Position II
Gruppenbefehlsfrequenz or the normal communication channel between all individual aircraft.

Position △
Nah-Flugsicherungsfrequenz or the communications between the pilot and ground control.

Position □
 Reichsjägerfrequenz or the ground combat control by the Jagdführer.

Bf 109 G-6/Y aircraft fitted with both the R7 kit and the FuG 16ZY could operate all four channels. Those aircraft with only the R7 kit could use only channels II and △. The "Y system" was a success in its early stage of operations; however, by 1944 even the ability to bring a maximum number of fighters to bear on a given bomber fleet was not enough unto itself.

Overleaf: Bf 109 G-6 of the NASM.

Bf 109 G-6/U2 found by advancing American troops at the Henschel Aero Engine Works, Attenbaum near Kassel.

During the autumn of 1944, as production of the Gustav rose to unprecedented levels, the Bf 109 G-6 was being replaced on the assembly line by the improved Bf 109 G-14. These new models were made available immediately to the Luftwaffe's fighter squadrons with the older Bf 109 G-6 models being passed to second-line units as trainer, liaison, and reconnaissance aircraft. Thus by December 10, 1944, only two day fighter units were equipped with the Bf 109 G-6: II./JG 2 under the Luftwaffen Kommando West commanded by Hptm. Georg Schröder based at Nidda, and III./JG 6 under Luft-

flotte Reich commanded by Maj. Helmut Kuhle based at Schwerin. In addition to the Bf 109 G-6, both of these units carried ample numbers of newer Bf 109 G-14 and Bf 109 K-4.

Several models of the Bf 109 G-6 appeared as operational on units status reports as late as February 1945, although the type was rapidly being withdrawn from all front-line units. One of the last units to operate the type was JG 51. On January 29, 1945, IV./JG 51 lost a Bf 109 G-6, W.Nr. 165 612, bearing a double chevron as staff identification emblem on its fuse-

lage. A typical figher group well known for its employment of the Bf 109 was JG 26. The following summary of the third squadron's (III./JG 26) aircraft usage over three and a half years is typical:

1942: Bf 109 F-4, FW 109 A-2, FW 190 A-4.

1943: Bf 109 G-3, Bf 109 G-4, Bf 109 G-6, FW 190 A-4, FW 190 A-5.

1944: Bf 109 G-6, Bf 109 G-14, Bf 109 K-4.

1945: Bf 109 G-14, Bf 109 K-4, FW 190 D-9.

Bf 109 G-6/N, W.Nr. 27 412, NH +VZ, fitted with underwing 20 mm cannon in addition to FuG 350 Naxos Z.

On June 27, 1943, a new fighter unit was activated expressly for an operational testing of a new form of night bomber interception known as "Wilde Sau" (Wild Boar). Designated JG 300, the unit was to send single-seat fighters among RAF night bombers in a free lance manner. Contact with enemy bombers was dependent entirely upon visual sighting, hoping that sufficient ground lighting would silhouette the bombers. Within a month three Gruppen of JG 300 based at Bonn-Hangelar, Oldenburg, and Rheine were joined by JG 301 at Neubiberg commanded by Maj. Helmut Weinrich, and JG 302 at Döberitz under Maj. Ewald Janssen for operational workup under the overall command of Oberstleutnant Hajo Hermann as part of 30. Jagddivision. Operations continued with considerable success over the next few months employing a variety of Gustav models. Early in 1944 a new device, known as FuG 350 Naxos Z, was mounted on several converted G-6/trop aircraft identified as the **Bf 109 G-6/N.** The FuG 350 was an electronic receiver which homed on the H2S radar of the RAF. By late 1943 night-fighter losses increased to a disproportionate level. Consequently, on March 16, 1944, 30. Jagddivision was disbanded. The few completed Bf 109 G-6/N models were never issued to JG 300, 301, or 302 but were sent instead to a specialized night-fighter unit. NJG 11.

This rare Bf 109 G-6/N is being tested with FuG 217J Neptun radar.

Bf 109 G-5/R2/AS, 12 +5F, attached to Aufkl. Gr. 14, the pilot of this reconnaissance aircraft was forced down by a U.S.A.A.F. Mustang pilot without firing a shot. A red cap over the nose cannon opening suggests the engine 20 mm cannon was not fitted. Poor quality of print is due to blurred composite made from movie film.

AS ENGINES

In an effort to increase the altitude capability of the Gustav, Damiler-Benz mated the larger diameter super-charger of its DB 603G to the DB 605A resulting in the DB 605AS (S=Sonder/Special). Preliminary tests were conducted in June 1944 with a Bf 109 G-5, W Nr. 26 108, SL +RR, fitted with the DB 605AS driving a VDM 9-12159A prop. A new deep-chin oil cooler, Fo 987, developed by SKF was adopted replacing the older and less favorable Fo 870. Generally tests were satisfactory, apart from some minor cowl sealing and exhaust penetration of the engine comparment which were easily corrected.[1] Aircraft selected to receive the AS engine included:

• Bf 109 G-5; G-5/U2; G-5/R2,
• Bf 109 G-6; G-6/U2; G-6/U4; G-6/R4,
• Bf 109 G-14; G-14/U4; G-14/U6.

Aircraft of the G-5, G-5/U2, G-6/U2, and G-6/R4 series received GM 1 powerboost while all marks of the Bf 109 G-14 routinely carried MW powerboost as standard. The most significant external feature common to all AS-powered versions was the new smoothly flared cowl which dispensed with the characteristic bulges of earlier models. An altered cowl was necessitated by the suitably curved left engine support arm having to clear the increased diameter of the supercharger as well as its increased width. Additionally, all AS-powered versions received the tall tail assembly, while most examples were supplied with the clear vision Erla-designed canopy. In most other respects AS models were similar to standard production G-5, G-6, and G-14 models.

[1]Radiator flap tests were conducted on June 22, 1944, with Bf 109 G-6/AS, W.Nr. 16 550, KT +DX powered by the DB 605 AS/V116, again with satisfactory results.

Two views of Erich K. Sommer's Bf 109 G-6/U2/AS which turned turtle while testing new bullet proof tires. Note the "T9" unit code just visible in the photo to the left indicating Versuchsverband OKL, a special test and evaluation unit attached to the High Command of the Luftwaffe.

A number of Bf 109 G-6 aircraft were acquired by the Western Allies; yet, only two survive (excluding two preserved in Finland)! On February 4, 1944, No. 1426 Flight, based at RAF Collyweston, received a crated Bf 109 G-6/trop carrying RAF code VX 101. Two months later, on April 10, 1944, it was reassembled and flown for evaluation although by this time its supercharger dust filter was removed. On May 19, 1944, the right undercarriage leg collasped during a landing accident at Thorney Island and the aircraft was reduced to spares on Sept. 26, 1944.

During the dark early hours of July 21, 1944, a German pilot attached to I./JG 301[2] flew his Bf 109 G-6/U2, W.Nr. 412 951, NS +FE, "White 16" into British hands at RAF Manston after accidentally flying a course reciprocal to that of his base in northern France. Later this aircraft was partially repainted, and was alloted Air Ministry code TP 814. Flown extensively by No. 1426 Flight, it subsequently crashed during takeoffon November 23, 1944, the pilot being uninjured.

Interestingly, another pilot of I./JG 301, Feldwebel Manfred Gromill, also mistaken-ly landed his Bf 109 G-6, W.Nr. 163 240, RQ +BK, at RAF Manston during the same morning after orbiting the field and flashing his navagation lights. Unlike the pilot of "White 16," Feldwebel Gromill choose a wheels-up landing. Thus by the end of 1944, no airworthy examples of the Bf 109 G-6 remained in England.

The United States Army Air Corps also acquired a few Bf 109 G-6 planes during the course of the war. Besides the example currently held by the National Air and Space Museum, a Bf 109 G-6/trop, W.Nr. 16 416, "White 9" was captured in the Mediterranean area and was received at Wright Field on July 14, 1943, becoming EB 102 (Evaluation Branch). As of August 10, 1944, it had logged 26 hours and was stored in Hanger 7 on an "active" status. By September 2, 1944, it had accummulated 29 hours and was scheduled for flight photos and angle-of-attack tests. The angle-of-attack tests continued through the 9th of September but by October 14, 14, 1944, it was no longer carried on active operations. Later, on October 24, it was located at Wright Field's Hilltop Lot slated for salvage and spare parts. Presumably this was done, for by March 17, 1945, it ceased to be carried within the listings. Some uncertainty exists concerning the identity of a Bf 109 G-6/trop which was involved in a landing accident at Wright Field during 1944. A U.S.A.A.F. pilot ground-looped a Bf 109 G-6/trop while avoiding a P-38 which was landing at the same time. Damage was such that it was decided not to salvage the aircraft. Possibly this aircraft was EB 102 but there is reason to believe that it was yet another Bf 109 G-6/trop. During mid-1944 a number of captured Axis aircraft participated in a nationwide tour under the heading "Shot From the Sky." One nonflying aircraft from this exhibit was a damaged Bf 109 G-6/trop once attached to JG 53. Upon completion of the tour, it is presumed that this aircraft was offered for salvage and subsequently broken up as no trace of it can be found.

[2]Some sources have identified this aircraft with I./JG 1. However as of 7/21/44, this day fighter squadron was equipped only with the Focke-Wulf FW 190 A-8. The red tail band was used from mid-1944 to early 1945 by three fighter groups: JG 1, JG 300, and JG 301. During February 1945, instructions were issued which allowed for only JG 1 to employ the red band while JG 300 and JG 301 respectively adopted blue-white-blue and yellow-red tail bands.

Bf 109 G-6/N probably attached to the staff of NJG 11.

Bf 109 G-6/U2/AS, another view of Erich K. Sommer's Gustav.

Bf 109 G-6/R6 serving with the Royal Hungarian Air Force.

Bf 109 G-6 of III./JG 1, Leewarden, Holland, mid-1943.

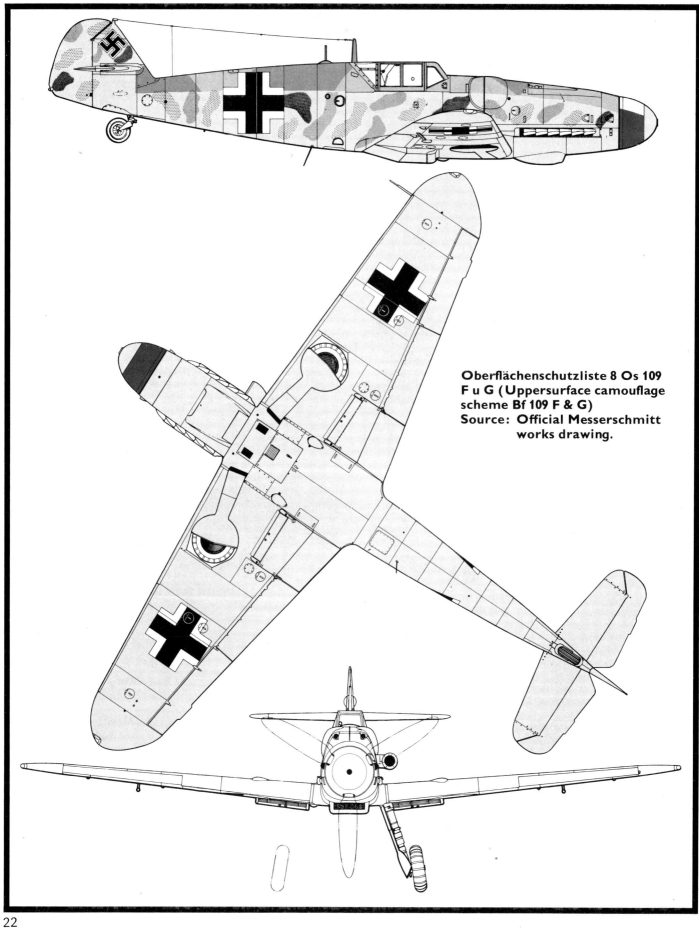

Oberflächenschutzliste 8 Os 109
F u G (Uppersurface camouflage
scheme Bf 109 F & G)
Source: Official Messerschmitt
works drawing.

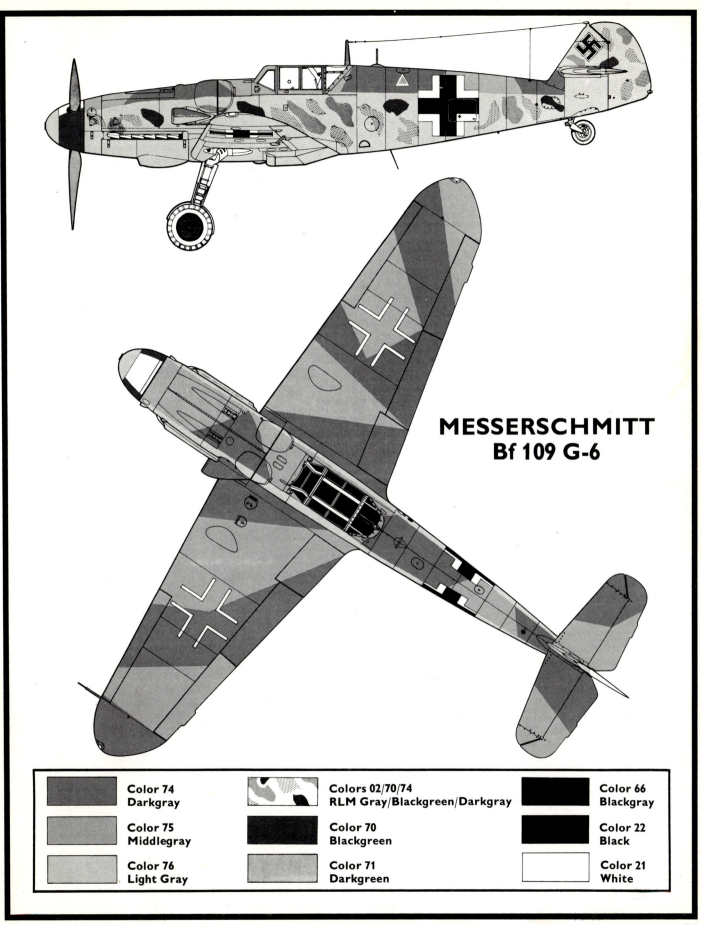

MESSERSCHMITT
Bf 109 G-6

Color 74 Darkgray	**Colors 02/70/74** RLM Gray/Blackgreen/Darkgray	**Color 66** Blackgray
Color 75 Middlegray	**Color 70** Blackgreen	**Color 22** Black
Color 76 Light Gray	**Color 71** Darkgreen	**Color 21** White

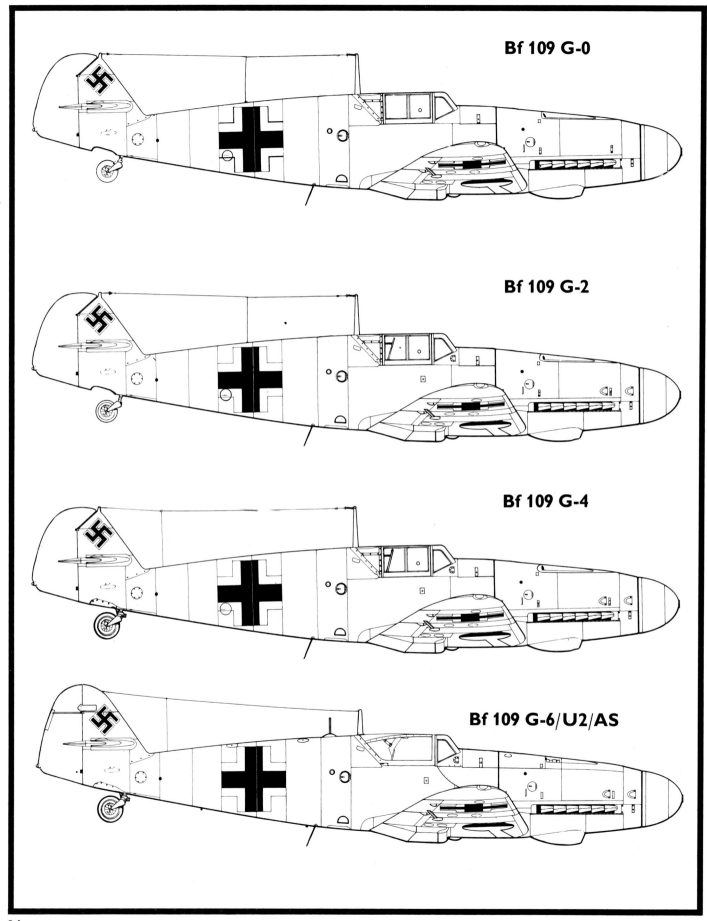

Bf 109 G-0

Bf 109 G-2

Bf 109 G-4

Bf 109 G-6/U2/AS

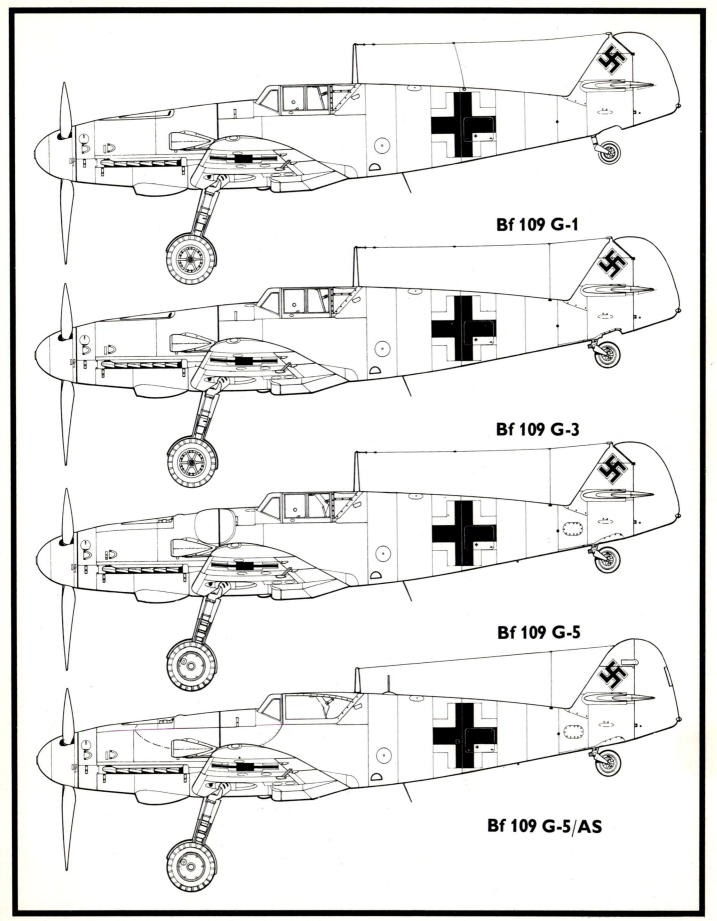

Bf 109 G-1

Bf 109 G-3

Bf 109 G-5

Bf 109 G-5/AS

Bf 109 G-6, W.Nr. 166 224, attached to a training unit bearing a yellow "97" on the rudder and being examined by American Officers at Nogent-le-Roi in 1945.

The DB 605A was the principal power-plant of the Gustav while the DB 605B and C engines were alternate engines restricted to the Bf 109 G-1 and G-2 series. The chart below equates 1 PS = 1 HP (PS = Pferdestärke/horse-power) but 1 PS more precisely equals 0.986 HP.

ENGINE	FUEL	AIRCRAFT ELIGIBLE FOR ENGINE
DB 605AM	C3	Bf 109 G-6, G-6/R2, G-8, G-14 (M=MW)
DB 605ASB	B4	Bf 109 G-5/R2, G-6, G-6/U4
DB 605ASC	C3	Bf 109 G-5, G-5/U2, G-6/U2, G-6/R4
DB 605ASM	C3	Bf 109 G-14, G-14/U4, G-14/U6 (M=MW)

DAILMER-BENZ DB 605A-C

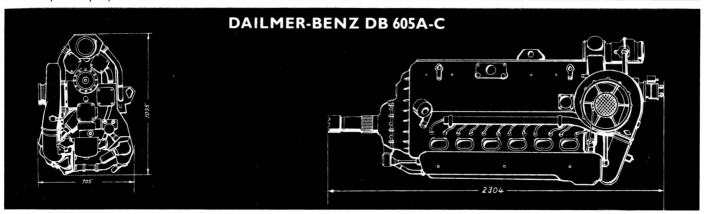

DAIMLER-BENZ ENGINE	DB 605A	DB 605B	DB 605C	DB 605AS
TYPE	12 Cylinder inverted Vee liquid cooled			
BORE	154mm (2⅛ in)			
STROKE	160mm (2⅜ in)			
COMPRESSION RATIO	7.3 : 1 left & 7.5 : 1 right			
PROP REDUCTION RATIO	1 : 1.685	1 : 1.875	1 : 2.060	1 : 1.685
LENGTH	2158.5mm (7 ft 0⅞ in)		2303.5mm (7 ft 6⅝ in)	
HEIGHT	1037.0mm (3 ft 4⅞ in)		1072.0mm (3 ft 6⅞ in)	
WIDTH	760.0mm (2 ft 5⅞ in)		793.0mm (2 ft 7¼ in)	
WEIGHT	756 kg (1.663 lb)			
TAKEOFF & EMERGENCY	1475 HP at 2800 rpm/1.42 ata/0 km (sea level)			1435 PS/2800 rpm/0 km
CLIMB & COMBAT	1310 HP at 2600 rpm/1.30 ata/0 km (sea level)			1275 PS/2600 rpm/0 km
MAX. CONT. CRUISE	1075 HP at 2300 rpm/1.15 ata/0 km (sea level)			1075 PS/2300 rpm/0 km
TAKEOFF & EMERGENCY	1355 HP at 2800 rpm/1.42 ata/5.6 Km (18,700 ft)			1200 PS/2800 rpm/8.0 Km
CLIMB & COMBAT	1250 HP at 2600 rpm/1.30 ata/5.7 Km (19,000 ft)			1150 PS/2600 rpm/7.8 Km
MAX. CONT. CRUISE	1080 HP at 2300 rpm/1.15 ata/54.4 Km (18,000 ft)			1050 PS/2300 rpm/7.7 Km
FUEL	B4 (87 octane)			
FUEL CONSUMPTION	509 lb /hr Max. Cont. Cruise at O km			521 lb /hr Max. Cont.C/O km

Left: The DB 605 A-1 of the NASM's Bf 109 G-6.

CAMOUFLAGE

The photograph above, depicting a Bf 109 G-6/R6, from the staff of JG 27, is typical of the Gustav. This scheme consisted of three lusterless grays sprayed in prescribed locations as shown on pages 22 and 23. Official employment of grays for Luftwaffe fighters began in 1940 and continued into mid-1944 when greens were specified for day fighters.

All undersurfaces were sprayed color 76 Lightgray which extended up the fuselage sides to a point slightly below the top decking. The uppersurfaces were sprayed in two shades of gray (Color 74 Dunkelgrau and Color 75 Mittlegrau) with a one inch overlap creating a soft edge. Along the fuselage sides including the vertical tailplane, a mottle of three colors was prescribed: Color 02 RLM Grau, Color 70 Swartzgrün, and Color 74 Dunkelgrau. Curiously, the spinner also received three colors: the forward cap in Color 76 Hellgrau, while the remainder was one-third Color 21 Weiss and two-thirds Color 70 Swartzgrün. The propeller blades received either Color 70 Swartzgrün or Color 71 Dunkelgrün, and like the spinner they were protected with a coat of clear lacquer known as Wasserhell 00, giving the finish a slight luster. The canopy exterior framing usually was sprayed Color 66 Swartzgrau since this was the color specified for armor plating and cockpit interiors.

The spinners often were sprayed a solid Blackgreen or were one-third White and two-thirds Blackgreen. Later, on July 20, 1944, instructions were issued which called for all fighters to have a distinctive black and white spiral motif applied to the spin-

ners. As production proceeded the three specified fuselage mottle colors often were reduced to either Dark Gray (74) and RLM Gray (02) or Blackgreen (70) and RLM Gray. However, by early 1944 the RLM Gray often was deleted altogether with the mottle consisting solely of either Dark Gray or Blackgreen. The interior of the aircraft received a clear lacquer or was left unprotected.

Aircraft operating over the Mediterranean area in North Africa were governed by the so-called "Tropical" regulations. This directive stated that all undersurfaces were to be painted in Color 78 Hellblau while all uppersurfaces were to be painted in Color 79 Sandgelb and Color 80 Olivgrün. The latter color (Olivegreen) was to be applied in a mottle over the Sandyellow although in actual practice this color was often deleted altogether. The Luftwaffe also employed a washable temporary camouflage paint but use of these paints was quite limited.

Foreign air arms using the Gustav generally retained German camouflage schemes with few exceptions.

MARKINGS

German national markings carried by the Gustav consisted of a 900 mm fuselage and underwing cross, a 1000 mm upperwing cross, and a 300 mm swastika on the fin.

Initially, early Gustavs (G-1, G-2) retained the style of cross employed by the earlier Fritz series as shown by the photographs

at the top of page 4. This style gave way to the simpler form shown in the lower photograph on page 3 (e.g. a/c DN +YK) but was soon standardized on that employed by the aircraft in the foreground in the same photograph (DN +YW). Underwing crosses initially were unchanged from the Fritz series but a simplified cross deleting the black trim was later specified. Additionally, the fuselage cross underwent another change as the war progressed, resulting in a deletion of the black center and replacing it with Color 74 Dark Gray (Color 80 for tropical types). However, there were instances when this was not done and the center simply amounted to the surrounding fuselage colors. The swastika was similar to that used by the F-series but discontinued the thin black outline. Some were given only a white outline swastika but this practice was not common. Newly completed aircraft usually were adorned with a factory code of four letters applied in a washable black paint along the fuselage side and underwing as shown on page 4. These letters, used during acceptance flights, normally being removed once the aircraft reached its assigned unit.

Other markings carried by the Gustav included a variety of tail bands, wing tip, tail, and nose colors in addition to an endless variety of unit insignia, rank, and replacement within a given unit. Readers desiring additional information are advised to seek works written by such authorities as Kenneth A. Merrick, Karl Ries Jr., J. Richard Smith and John D. Gallaspy, as the scope of such information exceeds the limits of this publication.

SWITZERLAND Bf 109 G-6, W.Nr. 163 243, J-704, one of twelve purchased in 1944.

FOREIGN SERVICE

Substantial numbers of the Gustav were employed by Germany's Axis partners during the war, nearly 700 being exported in addition to twelve sold to neutral Switzerland in 1944. Foreign production was undertaken by the Hungarian Wagonwerke at Budapest and Györ with foreign manufacture constituting approximately 650 aircraft. Only sixteen were completed by the I.A.R. plant at Brasnov, Rumania before the U.S.A.A.F. bombed the facility beyond immediate repair. Spain placed an order for the Gustav, but only twenty-five airframes were delivered. Following the war the Yugoslavian

Air Force acquired a few Bf 109 G-2 and G-6 models, most of these coming from Bulgaria as war reparations.

BULGARIA
Approximately 145 aircraft of the Bf 109 G-2 and G-6.

CROATIA
A small number of Bf 109 G-2, G-5, and G-6 models were delivered between July 1942 and February 1944.

FINLAND
From March 13, 1943, to mid-1944 a total of 162 Gustavs were delivered: Bf 109 G-1, G-2, G-6, and later models (see Monogram CU7).

HUNGARY
Fifty-nine Gustavs were received including: Bf

109 Ga-2, Ga-5, and G-6 models.

ITALY
Approximatley 156 Gustavs were received including: Bf 109 G-2, G-3, G-4, and G-6 models.

RUMANIA
Approximately 70 Gustavs were received from early 1943 to mid-1944 including: Bf 109 Ga-1, Ga-2, and G-6 models.

SLOVAKIA
Only about fifteen Gustavs including a few Bf 109 G-3 models but principally the Bf 109 G-6 were active from early 1943 until the uprising at Tri Duby.

SWITZERLAND
A total of fourteen Bf 109 G-6 models were operated by the Swiss but two were acquired when their German pilots landed in neutral Switzerland by navigational error.

BULGARIA Bf 109 G-6/Y, W.Nr. 166 133. Note U.S. flag on fuselage.

CROATIA Bf 109 G-5, attached to 15/JG52 "Croat Staffel."

FINLAND Bf 109 G-6/Y, W.Nr. 167 271, one of only two that survive intact in Finland today.

HUNGARY Bf 109 G-6/U2, W.Nr. 782205, W.0 +58, fitted with a lengthened tailwheel leg.

ITALY Bf 109 G-6/trop, one of about 148 G-6 models delivered.

RUMANIA Bf 109 Ga-2/R6 with late-war markings.

SLOVAKIA Bf 109 G-6, W.Nr. 161 717 crashed near Bumovce June 26, 1944.

On April 17, 1974, after two years of restoration work, the National Air and Space Museum rolled out its refurbished Bf 109 G-6 (ex FE-496) at Silver Hill, Maryland. Although records of this machine have disappeared, the author believes this example was acquired by U.S. Forces in Italy on July 25, 1944, in the Santa Maria area and is the same aircraft illustrated above. The pilot apparently brought his plane to this field purposely. Close examination reveals three features common to the NASM'S aircraft: both have the forward cowl vent scoop dented in the same location, both have the unusual combination of a tall radio mast with direction-finding loop, and finally, the ragged edge of the shell ejection chutes match perfectly. Since the manufacturer's plate had been removed, the serial number "160 163" was given conforming with others of this series. Restoration was guided by photographs of similar aircraft.

Above & below: Two views of one Bf 109 G-6/trop brought to the U.S. during 1943. Shown above it bears W.Nr. 16 416, "White 9" in addition to crude U.S. insignia. Later, upon arrival at Wright Field it was allocated Evaluation Branch code EB 102. The ultimate fate of this aircraft after March 17, 1945, is uncertain.
Left & Right: Instrument panel of the Bf 109 G-6 held by the NASM in Washington.

		Bf 109 G-6	Bf 109 G-6/R2	Bf 109 G-6/AS
Aircraft type				
Role		Fighter	Reconnaissance	Fighter
Seating		1	1	1
Surface area	m² (ft²)	16.05 -1.13 (173.34-66.20)	16.05-6.13 (173.34-66.20)	16.05-6.13 (173.34-66.20)
Maximum load area Takeoff weight	t (lb)	6.7/3.320 (72.4/7437)	6.5/3.300 (70.2/7392)	6.7/3.320 (72.4/7437)
Engine type		DB 605A	DB 650 AM	DB 605 ASB
Takeoff HP	PS (HP)	1475	1800	1435
Climb & Combat at 0 km	PS (HP)	1310	1240	1275
Climb & Combat at critical optimum altitude	PS (HP)	1250-5.8 (19,029 ft)	1250-5.8 (19,029 ft)	1150-7.8 (25,591 ft)
Maximum continuous 0 km	PS (HP)	1075	1020	1075
Maximum continuous maximum altitude	PS (HP)	1080-5.5 (18,045 ft)	1080-5.5 (18,045 ft)	1050-7.7 (25,263 ft)
Propeller type		VDM/9-12087	VDM/9-12087	VDM/9-12159
Diameter/blade number	m	3/3 (9 ft 10 in)	3/3 (9 ft 10 in)	3/3 (9 ft 10 in)
Fuel supply		Normal	MW 50	Normal
Weapons & Armor weight	t (lb)	0.135/0.078 (302 175)	0.135/0.046 (302/103)	0.135/0.078 (302/175)
Empty weight	t (lb)	2.268 (5,080)	2.268 (5,080)	2.293 (5,136)
Equipped weight	t (lb)	2.679 (6,001)	2.740 (6,138)	2.704 (6,057)
Crew weight	t (lb)	0.100 (224)	0.100 (224)	0.100 (224)
Fuel weight	t (lb)	0.296 (661)	0.295 (661)	0.296 (661)
Lubricants weight	t (lb)	0.033 (74)	0.033 (74)	0.033 (74)
Bombs	t (lb)	—	—	—
Ammunition	t (lb)	0.088 (197)	0.088 (197)	0.088 (197)
MW 50	t (lb)	—	0.063 (141)	—
Takeoff weight	t (lb)	3.196 (7,159)	3.320 (7,437)	3.221 (7,215)
Economy Cruising				
Estimated distance flown	km			
Range (safe)	km			
Optimum departure flight at altitude	km/h – km			
Optimum return flight at altitude	km/h – km			
Flight With High Performance Endurance				
Estimated distance flown	km (mi – ft)	560-6.0 (336-19,685)	550-6.0 (330-19,685)	550-8.4 (330-27,559)
Range (safe)	km			
Maximum cruise departure at altitude	km/h – km (mph – mi)	595-6.0 (369-19,685)	590-6.0 (336-19,685)	625-8.4 (388-27,559)
Maximum cruise return flight at altitude	km/h – km (mph – mi)	595-6.0 (369-19,685)	590-6.0 (366-19,685)	625-8.4 (388-27,559)
Maximum combat speed at ground level	km/h – km (mph – mi)	510-1260-0 (316-756-0)	498- (309-)	500-1235-0 (310-741-0)
Maximum combat speed at maximum altitude	km/h – km (mph – mi)	630-1230-6.6 (390-738-21,654)	628- -6.6 (389- -20,909)	648-1135-8.8 (402-681-28,871)
Maximum emergency speed at ground level	km/h – km (mph – mi)	530-1440-0 (329-864-0)	569- (353-)	520-1400-0 (322-840-0)
Maximum emergency speed at maximum altitude	km/h – km (mph – mi)	640-1340-6.6 (397-840-21,654)	566- -5.0 (350- -16,404)	660-1190-9.0 (402-714-29,528)
Optimum maximum cruise at ground level	km/h – km (mph – mi)	480-1075-0 (298-645-0)	469- (291-)	470-1050-0 (291-630-0)
Optimum maximum cruise at maximum altitude	km/h – km (mph – mi)	595-1080-6.0 (369-648-19,685)	590- -6.0 (366- -19,685)	625-1040-8.4 (388-625-27,559)
Service altitude – Takeoff weight	km – t (ft – in)	11.2-3.200 (35,482-7,168)	11.0-3.300 (34,848-7,392)	12.0-3.220 (38,016-7,213)
Climb to 6 km (19,685 ft) altitude	min	6.0	7.0	6.0
Rate of climb	m/s (ft – sec)	17.0 (56.1)	15.0 (49.2)	17.0 (56.1)
Takeoff distance	m (ft)	400 (1,320)	380 (1,254)	400 (1,320)
Maximum landing speed – Takeoff weight	km/h – t (mph – lb)	146-2.900 (91-6496)	150-3.000 (93-6.720)	146-2.900 (91-6496)
Armament		2 × MG 131 1 × MG 151/20	2 × MG 131 1 × MG 151/20	2 × MG 131 1 × MG 151/20

ADDENDUM:

IN ADDITION TO THE WERK NUMMERN LISTED ON THE INSIDE FRON COVER THE FOLLOWING SHOULD BE ADDED TO THE Bf 109 G-6: 180 000   230 000   442 000

SPECIFICATIONS   (common to all models)

Wing Span	9924mm	32 ft 6½ in
Length Overall	9020mm	29 ft 7⅛ in
Ground Height	2500mm	8 ft 2⅜ in
Elevated Height	3200mm	10 ft 5⅞ in
Ground to Canopy	2600mm	8 ft 6¼ in
Stabilizer Span	3000mm	9 ft 10 in
Prop Diameter	3000mm	9 ft 10 in
Wheel Track	2062mm	6 ft 9¼ in

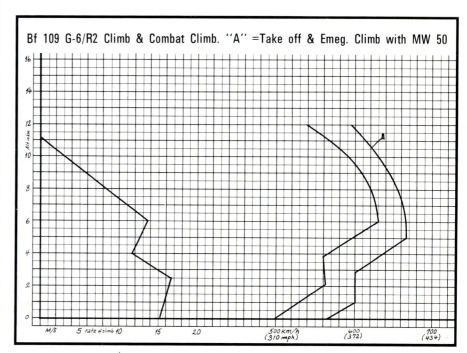

Bf 109 G-6/R2 Climb & Combat Climb. ''A'' =Take off & Emeg. Climb with MW 50